To Barbara

Thank you for ever
Through out life and
Been an Insperation

Love Margaret
Maxwell x

1

Hi,

I've never studied poetry; I have no huge qualifications in English language or literature. I'm simply a mother who writes for fun (to be fair I sometimes write to preserve my own sanity!)

I'm a mother to three 'proper' boys who spend their days fighting, arguing and well, just been boys really. I wouldn't change them for the world!

Back in 2008 I gave birth to my daughter Jayne Esther, she was my second child and sadly we lost her at 11 days old. Jayne had a CHD (Congenital Heart Defect) and despite her valiant effort and the efforts of the amazing staff at the Freeman Hospital it wasn't to be.

After Jayne's funeral I wrote the first poem I'd written in years 'One Final Kiss' you'll find it later in the book, I found poetry was a way for me to process things and so I started writing…

I tend to write about things I'd like to record, I've written poetry at request and just simply when something has inspired me.

This book has come about after years of nagging by family and friends to put my poems together for others to enjoy, on that note I hope you enjoy them……..

Thank you

Margaret x

This book is dedicated to:

All those who nagged me in to submission.

My family and friends for their support

My boys Peter, John and Mark, you are my inspiration

And those who have gone, but are never forgotten........

Contents

My Inspiration

I never thought I could be a poet
Though I think in rhyming couplets all the time
I thought poets were so clever
That they were big posh people so refined

Then I found when bad things happened
I needed to find a way to cope
I needed a way to get me through it
A way to stop me losing hope

I found some paper and a pencil
I made some notes of what I'd say
If I could speak to all the people
Who'd helped me through my darkest days

The friends and family who held me closer
Who listened and who dried my tears
Both at the time and ever since then
At random stages throughout the years

The passing strangers who at times
Paused to give me their support
A cheer, a prize for a fundraising raffle
A cash donation or tickets bought

When times are hard, I look around me
And I think of those throughout the years
<u>You are</u> my poetic inspiration
<u>You're</u> why I sit here writing, fighting tears

The Juicy Duck

If you head down Morpeth

Go down the riverside

See the local wild fowl

As gracefully they glide

Up and down the Wansbeck

And depending on your luck

You may hit on a good day

And see the 'juicy duck'

It glides round with the others

It's head held oh so high

That's NOT a duck, I hear you say

It's a SWAN you cry!

And yes you're right it's not a duck

It is indeed a swan

But my four year old said 'juicy duck'

And although I know he's wrong

His little face was oh so proud

Of this new bird, that he'd found

So next time that you're down there

See if the JUICY DUCK's around!!

What's a Family?

What's a family? I hear folk say

It's the people who put up with me every day!

Its' not just blood, but friends as well

When you're worried, it's those you can tell

They're willing to listen to all your grumbles

Over a bowl full of ice-cream or a dish full of crumble!

They're the ones that you hold, close in your heart

Where time doesn't matter, nor your distance apart

Your're there for each other, come hell or high water

Whether a mother, a father, a son or a daughter

A brother, a sister, a husband or wife

Related by blood or good friends for life!

What's a family? I hear folk say

It's the people I love each and every day!!

Grandad.

When I was just a girl
And I sat upon his knee
I used to love the tales
My Grandad told to me
Tales from when he was young
And he grew up by the Clyde
Of hide and seek with his siblings
All the places they would hide

Of going on the Waverley
The last great paddle steamer
Of working from so young
No time to be a dreamer
From braiding horses hair
To win the local show
To working for the railway
How quick he had to grow

When he met and fell in love
As he grew into a man
The rest they say is history
That girl he loves my Gran
With Gran right by his side

Although times could be tough
Getting them through it all
Their love's always been enough

Now Gran and Grandad have gone
Moved on to a higher plain
I wish I could go to Heaven
And bring them back home again
My head fills with memories
Of the tales my Grandad would tell
I pass them on to my boys
So they'll know my hero as well

The First Men

They were the first men to ever love me

The first men I ever loved

My Daddy and my Grandad

Surely sent from God above

They were there to chase my fears away

They'd take my hand

You'd hear them say

Don't you worry, don't you cry

We're both here so dry your eyes

Always ready to fight my corner

Always ready to keep me safe

No matter what was coming, each and every day

Each year as I get older

Though my Grandad had to go

I'm privileged to have known him

And I dearly miss him so

My Dad's still right beside me

Through every battle that I fight

I love him with every breath I take

And I thank God for him each night

Guiding Home

Losing your baby is wrong, you see

I know this for sure coz it happened to me

My girl went to Heaven, with loved ones above

But I know she's with me, I still feel her love!

I know I can't hold her, nor hug her so tight

But I feel her with me, morning and night!

She's there when I wake, each day with a smile

She's here on my journey, through life all the while

She's watching her brothers and cousins at play

She's right there beside them, protecting each day

I know they'll be safe, with Jayne as a guide

Through life's winding road, temptation each side

She'll watch every moment, to see they don't stray

Through life's little hiccups, each n every day

And if life should hurt them, leave them feeling alone

Be it brother or cousin, she'll guide them all home

Boys Will Be Boys!!

Boys will be boys, or so they say

I love mine more, each passing day

How do you cope, with three of them?

I close my eyes and count to ten

If ten don't work I count some more

And then thank goodness, I don't have four!!!

Typical lads, or so they say

With a cheeky nudge and a wink they play

Cheeky smiles, on their cheeky faces

You can tell they're going places

Usually where they shouldn't be

So I thank goodness there's only three!!!

Counting Blessings

At night when I quietly sit
And contemplate my day
I give thanks that I was blessed
That you three came my way

You fill my days with endless fun
Though there's time when sadness creeps in
You're all very good at squashing it
Scrunching up and putting in bins

We've walked for miles catching Pokémons
Drank hot chocolate in Central Bean
We've gone to places I've never gone
Seen sights that I've never seen

We've walked through the woods
Along the shore, searching for pirate gold
With you three boys keeping me on my toes
The years pass, but I could never feel old

The time will sadly come, I guess

When you're too big to be holding my hand

But then your hand will be replaced

By your kids holding hands with their Gran!

It's Not Fair!

It's not fair!
But you're tired and you're weary
You need to rest your head
Come on now my little lad
Get ready and off to bed

It's not fair!
Your eyes are almost closing
Although you're putting up a fight
Come and give me cuddles now
And a gentle kiss goodnight

It's not fair!
It's getting late my little lad
The day is nearly done
Go and dream of what we'll do
When the brand new day does come

It's not fair!

We'll get up in the morning

And have adventures all the day

But first you need to go to bed

And sleep your tiredness away

It's not fair!

Yet your eyes are closing

And you're nodding off to sleep

I'll carry you carefully up to bed

And safe with my love you'll keep

Why?

Why do you fight morn till night?

Why do you nip, punch and tease?

As siblings, as brothers just show some love!

I'm begging you please, oh please!

Why do you feel the need to jump?

From over here to over there

Why must you make each other cry?

Why do you feel the need to scare?

Why can't you just sit quietly?

And play a game together

Why must you fight and argue?

No matter where, or what the weather

Why can't you walk? When you're in the house

Why do you always run?

Why do you constantly need to shout?

Why can't you quietly have fun?

Why do you make me feel unreasonable?

When I ask you to calm down

All this been said I've got to say

It's TOO quiet when you're not around!

Winters Children

The cold frozen air it clings so hard

As winters children stand their guard

Dagger tipped icicles hang all around

As winters children stand their ground

Snowflakes softly start to flutter

As winters children quietly mutter

Dark winters nights early fall

As winters children begin to call

In warm beds we try to sleep

As winters children coldly creep

You wake up startled at a sound

As winters children gather round

The fear it screams within your head

As winters children strike you dead.

Sum of all Fears

The sum of all fears, it's not two plus two

It's what scares me and what scares you

From heights to spiders and all that's between

It's the most gruesome monster you've ever seen

It's what wakes you up, in the darkest of nights

It creeps up behind you, to give you a fright

It makes spooky noises, when you're all alone

It taps on the window, it calls on the phone

The monster in closet or down in the cellar

It shies from the sunshine, it loves stormy weather

It follows you home at night when it's dusky

When it calls your name, its voice is quite husky

It creeks in the trees, it scratches on glass

It growls in the corner, each time you pass

The sum of all fears, it's not two plus two

It's what scares me and what scares you

Forbidden Fruits

The cherries hung in bunches
All over the huge great tree
Bright jewels of crimson red
For all of us to see

The fruit it was forbidden
You dare take not one
Then one morning you'd awake
And the fruit would be all gone

But after lunch that Sunday
The most delicious cherry pie
If I said it wasn't worth the wait
Well then, that would be a lie

With homemade bread all toasted
And cherry jam on top
You'd happily sit for breakfast
And scoff the whole damn lot

All these memories of childhood

They sure do make you smile

N' for stuff made with Gran's forbidden fruit

I'd walk the extra mile

The Impossible Kiss

The kiss that is impossible
To forget from then as now
The final kiss your Mother placed
So gentle on your brow

A warm feeling that is always there
With memories come to mind
Of a woman who loved you always
And a happy family time

When the days are darkest
When life is hard to bear
Remember how it felt and know
Your Mother's always there

It maybe you can't see her now
Stood right by your side
But I know that she will take your hand
She'll always be your guide

The kiss that is impossible
To forget from then as now
The final kiss your Mother placed
So gentle on your brow......

Lucy, Lipstick, Glasgow

Lucy looked into the mirror
Her lipstick to apply
She'd stopped a night in Glasgow
On her way to Skye

She'd been to see a concert
At Glasgow's SEC
A trip down Sauchiehall Street
And a pit stop for her tea

She'd hopped aboard the Waverley
The last great paddle steamer
A trip along the Clyde
She'd always been a dreamer

Along passed Greenock, Gourock
Right up the Kyles of Bute
With whisky flowing freely
She was nissed as a pewt!

Dragon, Warrior Princess and a Bottle with a Cork

The dragon flared his nostrils

Letting out a puff of smoke

He'd said a double brandy

Not just a glass of coke

The bartender he apologised

As he took the bottle down

He removed the cork and took a sniff

His eyes went round and round

Are you sure you want a double?

It'll put hairs upon your chest

Just pour it man the dragon said

Leave the bottle, I'll drink the rest

The warrior princess entered

Hey dragon, you fancy a whirl

The dragon looked up gobsmacked

As the princess gave a twirl

They danced the light fantastic

All over the kitchen sink

And when they were both knackered

They sat down and had a drink!

Family and Footbaal

Me Mam she was a lovely lass

Alas she deed too young

Me Fatha he's a cracker jack

He's loads n loads ov fun

He tecks wi ti the footbaal

Doon by the riva Wear

Wa Mackems see its frond upon

By loads ov folk roond here

Wa colours red n white ye see

Wa jorseys on the line

Most folk roond here are black n white

Tha teams doon by the Tyne

Nuw footbaals not just a game

It IS a way of life

And when the Mackems beat the Geordies

Wey a git a load ov strife

Teck this year the Premier League

Leicester win it fair n square

The Toon went doon, we bided up

Ye shud hev hord thum swear

Am ganna miss the darby days

A dee enjoy the banta

Away days at Sid James's park

Drinkin vodka mixed wi fanta.

Homework

But a divint want to dee it

Even though a knaa a shud

Homework is si borin'

Ooo di ye think a cud?

Just say the durg, he ate it

Chowed it aal up for a snack

A cudn't hand it in then

It's not like aa cud get it back

Div ye think Sor wud be mad then?

Wi steam cummin oot his ears

Div ye think a'd get detention?

Yi'd hear me Mutha shoot from here!

Me Mam shi'd not be happy

Shi really wud be mad

Nd what wud meck it warsera?

Wey a knaa shi'd tell me Dad

Me Fatha he'd gan mental

A'd get a clip aroond me ear

So a guiss that ansas me question

A'd betta dee me homework here!

The Blood Dripped

The blood dripped from the knife
And landed on the floor
Where the cold, dead body
Writhed and twitched no more

The eyes were blank and open
The throat was cut right through
She looked at her handy work
Now what was she to do?

Why couldn't she remember?
Why it had all begun?
She turned and saw the hook
Where his intestines now hung

She made her way unto the fire
To warm her frozen heart
Why did the argument begin?
Why did the violence start?

She felt the cold sharp knife

Dripping fast congealing blood

Looked into the mirror

And slit her throat where she stood

What Happened Next?

Old Mr Smith
From thirty four
Situated on the
Second floor

Heard a thud
And a muffled call
As something upstairs
On the floor did fall

He paused
And looked up at the ceiling
Something had happened
He had a feeling

Although quite what
He didn't know
He shrugged as the bangs
Started to slow

Later he'd wish
He'd followed his feeling
When blood started dripping
Right through his ceiling

The blood was thick
Bright red and runny
It brought with it a smell
That was kind of funny

The smell of death
From the upstairs flat
He called the police
They could deal with that

The police arrived
To take a look
And found intestines
Hung from a hook

With bits of body
Strewn with great care
Some over here
And some over there

By the fire, the body
Of a woman did land
Eyes dark and blank
A knife in her hand

Upon a table
Not too far away
In the neatest of writing
A note did say....

He made his choice
His die was cast
I knew his affair
Would never last

He's played many games
Within my head
But mines the last laugh
Coz now he's dead!

My Memories are Mine.

You want my home?

Take it

All the money I own?

Take it

The clothes from my back?

Take them

My coat and my hat?

Take them

The material possessions that I own

My car, my clothes, my family home

Are not what is most important to me

They are replaceable, just look and see

The things with which I will never part

I carry with me in my head and my heart

They're memories of years gone by

Of the times we laughed and the times we cried

Of what's been done, friends and family

Those still here and those gone you see

Memories that can't be replaced

Of the good times and bad times that we've faced

Without my memories I couldn't go on

My mother, my daughter, my grandparents gone

No memories at all? I wouldn't be there

My boy they would see but a ghost in my chair

So the car and the cash, help yourself to the lot

But my memories I'll keep, coz they're all that I've got

Memory Tears

A tear is but a memory
That escapes from your eye
But that doesn't mean, you
Should be afraid to cry

Your memories are backed up
Within your head and heart
And they'll be with you always
You never have to part

Memories of being a child
Running wild and free
Through the years of growing
Deciding what to be

The first time that you fell in love
And held your sweethearts hand
Of days spent at the beach
Building castles in the sand

Of the day that you were married
To your greatest love in life
He became a husband
And you became a wife

When your tiny baby left
Their footprints in your heart
That's when you became a Mam
And family life did start

Of the days when you felt proud
As you watched your baby grow
Your eyes shining bright
And your cheeks all aglow

So when you think of all these times
And the tears they start to flow
Remember that they'll stay with you
Your memories won't go

Seasons

Spring it turns to summer
Autumn, winter will follow too
Life is like the seasons
Always changing, forever new

Our spring is our youth and childhood
When everything starts to grow
We learn so much so quickly
And the first buds of flowers do show

As quick we approach the summer
Our adult life begun
We meet our soulmate if we're lucky
And spend many years in the sun

We feel our love deeper than ever
As the leaves change colour and fall
We snuggle up warm with family and love
And autumn comes to call

As life and the year gets later
The cold winds of winter do blow
The days are darker but with fun to be had
With our sweetheart and children in snow

As the years end comes, we reflect
On the good times that we've shared
With family around us, a heart full of love
And our soulmates always there

Home

It's true what they say

No matter where you roam

When you find a place, no THE place

You know that you are home

It doesn't really matter

How far and wide you've been

All the places you have visited

All the many things you've seen

When you find that special place

That you carry in your heart

It's a bond that holds forever

Even if you're miles apart

Your home's your home you see

As it pulses in your veins

And it doesn't matter what you do

In your mind it still remains

So go out and see the world

Visit each and every place

But know at home you'll always have

Your own special little space

If I Were.....

If I were..... a butterfly
A fluttering on the breeze
I'd stop to smell the flowers
I'd sit among the trees
Beautiful, bright, rainbow wings
Would carry me everywhere
I'd flit from place to place you see
Without a worldly care

If I were..... a tiny mouse
A scuttling across the ground
I'd hide from all the birds of prey
A flying all around
I'd be as quick as lightning
I'd be a clever mouse
I might just find a crack or hole
And hide inside your house

If I were a..... long thin snake

A slithering on the grass

I'd sunbathe in the morning sun

Watching tiny creatures pass

When lunchtimes here my tummy rumbles

And pangs of hunger come

I creep up behind the tiny creatures

And bite them on the bum

The Volcano

The volcano lay quiet
Silent in her thoughts
Her last eruption distant
But now
Deep within
She grumbles
She grumbles and rumbles
Rumbles and grumbles
As the pressure mounts
And the magma deep inside
Starts to rise
Slowly
Slowly
It builds
Until
With force
She rips apart
Lava flowing
Hot and steaming
In rivulets gleaming down her side

From her cap flies

Ash and pumice

Hot magma splashes

Vicious, uncaring

It claims and ravages

Anything in its way

Stifling, choking

Ash and pumice

Encompassing all…

A Special Invitation.

It landed on the doorstep

On the twelfth of May

An invitation for us all

To share your special day

It made us all excited

It made me start to dream

What to wear? Skirt or pants?

In lemon, pink or cream?

I'm going to have to look

For what? I'm not quite sure

I only know it needs to be

Chic and haut couture

We've prayed to higher powers

Our fingers crossed it's true

We hope on hope God does it

And makes the sun shine through

We hope your time is special

In every single way

And thank that you're allowing us

To share your Wedding Day…

Quilters

The clicking of needles
The pulling of thread
These ladies make quilts
That keep you warm in bed

From scraps of material
Bought found, new or fade
These magical ladies have
Beautiful patchwork things made

With bright coloured threads
And a lot of hard work
It takes hours to do
These women don't shirk

Their stitches are tiny
The results are just fab
The most beautiful cushions
The most fabulous bags

The outcomes are amazing

Just come take a look

These folk are fantastic

Well, they are in my book

The Truth Of It All

Just wait till we cover her over
We don't want you getting upset
Heart surgeries so brutal and difficult
You don't wanna see the great hole in her chest

Don't be alarmed by the beeping and buzzing
The flashing lights and the constant noise
The needles, the swabs and the sick bowls
Imagine they're Hospital toys

She's asleep, she's sedated and drowsy
So don't expect much movement at all
If you're worried or have any questions
We're here watching over, just call

It's hard when you first see your baby
All tubes and wires and beeps
It's hard not being able to hold them
So safe in your arms you can keep

But you walk into that room, your eyes open
And believe me, you really don't see
The machines, the tubes and the wires
It's just the baby you love, and thee

A Broken Heart

Sat in a room
Serious faces
Bring your world
Crashing down

A baby, the baby
The one in your womb
Perfect in every way
Except
A broken heart

Your world stops turning
You feel your heart break
A silent tear
Moves quietly
Slowly
Down your cheek

WHY ME?
Your mind cries
In anguish
WHY ME?

No answer
No-one hears

Your cry

The silent tears
Keep falling

A mother's heart
Keeps breaking

A Letter from Heaven.

When I died you cried,
Tears like endless rain.
I wanted so much to hold you,
To come back from Heaven again.

But Heaven's a place that's forever,
And I had to watch from afar.
My friend know my love is for always,
That I'm drying your tears from a star.

Please know that I'll always be watching,
From my seat in Heaven above.
With arms that are ready to catch you,
To keep you safe with love.

My friend don't be scared as time passes,
I'm in your heart every day.
Live your life to the full and enjoy it,
I'm here by your side, I won't stray.

Heaven's Tears

Rain falls like Heaven's tears
From those we've missed o' the years
Those who've gone too soon before
That we miss now forever more
When they went out heart did break
The pain the grief so hard to take
As years pass by and times move on
We come to accept that they have gone
Although we wish them here today
We've learned to cope in many ways
We gaze at photos on the shelf
We hold them deep within our self
Happy memories will never go
Though the sadness ebbs and flows
Dry days come the tears they stop
And coloured flowers start to pop
As good memories return to mind
Of all the happy family times
So when Heaven's tears fall from above
Know those missing send their love

One Final Kiss.

Today was the day of our last kiss goodbye,
Rain fell from heaven, like tears from my eyes
Sat in the church, though kind words were spoken
Little comfort to me and my heart that was broken
A mother should never live through pain like this
I couldn't have done it, but for your brother's kiss
He held my hand, looking at me with love
He told me you'd look down on us all from above
From your Grandma's arms you'd be watching us all
Ready to catch us if we should fall
Balloons they hang in the sky up above
Red and white balloons with our message of love
Up to heaven they'll fly, where you can catch them and play
Knowing we will be together someday
Till then sleep tight with the angels above
Safe in the knowing, you have our love
Years will pass and times move on
I still can't believe my daughter has gone
In my heart you always will be
My brave beautiful girl born with CHD

Man and Boy

Man and boy all these years
Worked together through their fears
Life's ups and downs, smiles and frowns
They wouldn't let life get them down
They made the best of situations
Helped each other, no hesitation
And when life got truly tough
As father and son they had their love
In the mines they worked the line
Breathed fresh air together, at home time
Coal and soot, big hobnail boots
They were not posh, no expensive suits
They worked every day from dawn till dusk
Mining coal for all of us
If things went wrong as they sometimes do
Their family's heartbreak, what to do?
The mine collapses, sirens sound
Man and boy are never found.....

Coal Tubs

The empty tub stands in the siding
No longer used for hauling coal
The days of fossil fuel is passing
The open fire is growing old

But what of the tales the tub could tell
If we only took the time
To sit and listen 'bout days gone past
And the lads who grafted down the mine

Of jam sarnies saved for later
All wrapped up in greaseproof paper
Your Davy lamp shining bright
To light your safe way home tonight

Short, strong ponies, all harnessed up
Heave and pull the heavy tubs
Tubs filled with dusty, pitch black coal
To keep us warm and fight the cold

But now the tubs are standing empty
No longer used through these long years
The pitman's job is slowly dying
As time moves on, seems no-one cares

The lads that've been lost over time
In big disasters down the mine
Colliery villages torn apart
Families left with broken hearts

If only the tubs could talk awhile
I'm sure we'd laugh, cry and smile
With all the tales that they could tell
Of working in that cold, dark hell.......

The Posing Puffin

You're vain came the Seagull's call
From high up on the harbour wall
No I'm not the Puffin cried
'Twas the scene that caught my eye

So why for hours have you been stood?
The scenery's really not that good
Coz, when, looking at the lighthouse
I'm pretty sure I spied a mouse

A mouse? The Seagull laughed
You must think that we're all daft
You're posing, why not tell the truth?
Oh boy the joys of being a youth

With nowt to do and nowt to say
You can simply laze your days away
The Puffin puffed, the Puffin huffed
Then jumped in the sea, he'd had enough!

Kentish Memories

In the Kentish countryside
Where the trees are so beautifully green
There stands a bridge made of stone
The strongest you've ever seen

The bridge it crosses the river
As it meanders round the bend
The great old trees stand tall and strong
We'd climb them now and then

We'd cross the bridge on our way to church
On Sundays, before and after
And in the summer we'd plodge a while
Oh boy you'd hear our laughter

We'd fish along the river bank
Throw pooh sticks over the side
We'd watch the ducks and swans
As gracefully they'd glide

Though its many years, since I was young
I remember running late
We'd run across the old stone bridge
And climb over the five bar gate

So many memories I could share
But I don't know where to start
Of the bridge, the river, the trees and gate
All things I carry in my heart

The Lighthouse and the Boat

With the crashing of the waves

Upon the rocky shore

Mother Nature's anger

Could be contained no more

Somewhere in the distance

A small and worried boat

Struggles hard, with all its might

Just to stay a float

The waves are getting wilder

As they drive it to the shore

If it crashes on the rocks

The small boat will be no more

Then somewhere in the darkness

It hears a gentle call

Don't you worry little boat

I am here, you will not fall

I will use my light to guide you

Through the rough and violent swell

Just you follow it with caution

And I'll make sure that you're well

The little boat said thank you

I was getting so afraid

But with a friend beside me

I'm feeling much more brave

The lighthouse smiled back at him

Said don't you worry, that's alright

I am proud to be here helping

Passing ships on stormy nights

Seasons Sun Set

Bright yellow ball of fire

Amidst an orange glow

Upon a hill in the distance

Skeletal trees do grow

As dusk falls upon the landscape

A lonely bird does call

Over weeks of colder weather

Autumnal leaves did fall

Wind blows leaves down the hillside

And along the valley floor

As autumn slowly turns to winter

And summer is no more

Then snow will fall, the scene will whiten

Winter does bluster cold

Around the trees upon the hillside

Children laugh and play in the snow

The world turns the seasons change

Spring will come again

We give thanks for fresh spring colours

Through Mother Nature ascend

As spring changes the sun does shine

When summer returns at last

But all too soon autumn calls

Again summer's a thing of the past

Memories and Reflection

A woodland walk, on a quiet day
A moment of reflection, in snowdrop glade
The sound of leaves, crunched under feet
A fallen tree, a perfect seat

Memories flooding, back to mind
Of growing up and great fun times
Times spent in the treehouse, we once had
Lovingly built, for us by Dad

The years have passed, they've not been kind
Our treehouse broken, parts hard to find
But in my mind, my memories clear
Resolutions made, to return joy here

To clear the area, all around
Allowing natures beauty, to be found
To be enjoyed by all, and one
And shared in future, with my Son….

My Boy

My boy has packed his kit and gone

A mother's heart feels so alone

I can't believe it's come to this

They said it's over for Christmas

Recruiting drives still going on

All the men packed up and gone

To war they go, I feel so low

I prayed they wouldn't have to go

But go they did, my husband, my son

I feel the battles just begun

Our troop some fallen at the Somme

The war keeps raging on and on

My men have gone, my biggest fear

This won't be over for New Year

Bullets!

Bullets flying
Bodies lying
Friends and comrades
Lying!
Dying!

War's not big
War's not clever
Families split
Some forever!
A shout
A cry
A loud explosion
It's hard to survive
In this commotion

Friends hit the ground
Breathing their last
Here on the front line
Bullets whizz past

Every morning
I hope and I pray
The conflict will end
Maybe today??
Maybe soon
That day at last
My family around me
The war will have past!!

<u>Where's My Daddy?</u>

Where's my daddy? The children call

He's gone to war to protect us all

Far away in distant lands

Brothers in arms hand in hand

Our husbands, dads, brothers stand

To fight for peace in our fair land

Where's my daddy? The children call

He's gone to war to protect us all

Friends are dying, bullets flying

Everyday families crying

As news comes through of soldiers dying

We hope, we pray but feel like crying

Where's my daddy? The children call

He fell in the war, God help us all!

Where's my daddy? The children cry

How do you answer, with tears in your eyes?

Hush little baby, please don't cry

Daddy has met with the man in the sky!!

Never Forget!

Their blood was spilt on foreign lands

And angels took them by the hand

They gave their lives for all of us

NEVER FORGET!

Some came home and fought some more

The pain they felt

The horrors they saw

THEY WILL NEVER FORGET!

As the sun will rise on another Armistice Day

We mourn the loss

The heartaches and pray

WE WILL NEVER FORGET!

War Isn't Cool

On Armistice Day
Each year in November
We all bow our heads
And those lost we remember

All the brave troops who fought
In battles so hard
Who laid their lives down
Away from families so far

All those left behind
With the pain and the loss
The child with no father
They know what war really cost

As the last post does sound
And the bugle silent falls
We'll all shed a tear
At the memories it calls

Of photos and film
We all saw at school
Images showing the truth
That war isn't cool

So this year in November
As the last post does sound
I hope people remember
The sense of loss that they've found

The sadness, the loss
The real pain of war
It's not big, it's not clever
We've been there before

So let's all make a pact
As a world make a rule
All the fighting will stop
Remember, war isn't cool.....

To the Fallen Soldier at the Somme….

You didn't know me
But you fought for me
I wasn't born back then
You didn't know us
But you fought for us
Lying wounded among dying men

In a field in France
On the War's Western Front
A battle that lost thousands
Truth be told
In trenches and on no-man's land
We lost so many hearts of gold

Where the ground is red with blood
Down by the river Somme
The river flows so quietly
Filled with tears as war goes on
Men and boys suffer in agony
From the torture of gas and wounds
Sit up world and take notice
We need the wars to end soon

It was the war to end all wars
If only that were true
For as these hundred years have past
We've lost so many men like you
I'd like to thank you for your bravery
For giving me today
Please know that I'll remember you
And what you gave for us all that day

Winter Walk

A walk along the river bank
It's Mother Nature you have to thank
As ducks do lazily glide on past
With peace and quiet you want to last

The smell of damp within the air
Makes you realise you just don't care
You don't care if rain starts to fall
Or if in your bones cold creeps and crawls

The cool misty air, the pattering sound
As rain it falls upon the ground
The leaves still missing from the trees
Blown near and far on last year's breeze

Warm sun's a distant memory
Winter's here for all to see
Mother Nature's stark grey gown
Discarded leaves still strewn around

But soon the sun will start to show
And in its warmth, small bulbs will grow
The nights will shorten and days grow long
As we greet the warmth of a summer's sun

The Snowman

The Snowman stood in frosty air

The wind blew cold but no-one cared

He pulled his scarf tighter round

And his hat harder down

I'm freezing, said snowman Hugh

It's enough to turn your snowballs blue

No-one seems to understand

They wear mitts upon their hands

So when the kids they start to freeze

They go inside out of the breeze

They sit by fires in a huddle

But if I did that I'd be a puddle.......

The Gift

The gift it lay unopened
Down by the Christmas tree
Covered in beautiful paper
It looked so special to me

Not knowing where it came from
Or who had put it there
I went across and pick it up
With the utmost care

The tag it was so sparkly
Shaped just like a star
I reached to turn it over
To see if it travelled from far

The name on the bottom, surprising
As I stared at it there in my hand
Merry Christmas from up here in Heaven
With all of my love, from Mam

A quiet tear escaped me
For I knew that Heaven was far
But it made my Mam feel much closer
As I know she watched from a star

Nativity

Mary travelled to Bethlehem
Upon a donkey's back
The order came from Herod
They had to go, and that was that

The journey it was tiring
As pregnant Mary found
They looked for rooms a hiring
There were no rooms at all around

A stable she was offered
By an innkeeper who did care
He said it's warm and dry pet
You can have your baby there

Upon the hill the shepherds
Quietly sat 'round
When angels did appear to them
Releasing glory 'pon the ground

As far away wise men
Beheld a bright new star
With gold, myrrh and frankincense
'Pon camels and travelled afar

With long journeys now behind them
Arrive the shepherds and the kings
At the stable to meet baby Jesus
With beautiful gifts they bring

Baby Jesus is oh so peaceful
As in the manger he sleeps
The cattle are a lowing
As safe in the stable they keep

A Family Christmas.

As families come together, around the Christmas tree

Children all excited, to see what there maybe

Their happy little faces, bring back memories

Of times we were together, one big happy family

Time it's been a passing, the years keep rolling on

I wake up every morning, forgetting that you're gone

Heaven needed angels, God took the very best

To sit with him above, watching over all the rest

As Christmas morn approaches, you're never far from mind

All my family that is missing, at this very special time

So we'll do it all again, like we have for all these years

Putting smiles on faces, hiding all the tears

Sitting round the table, bittersweet memories

Of times we were together, around the Christmas tree

A Poetic Christmas Carol

The ghost of Christmas Past
Shuddered and looked around
The snow was falling thick and fast
As it settled on the ground

Ebenezer Scrooge was cowering
Within his great, grand bed
He was petrified and mortified
Thinking he was surely dead

I've come to show your errored ways
Said the ghost of Christmas Past
Then maybe you may make a change
A change that is to last!

A lasting change?! Ebenezer cried
Please just leave me here alone
I'll do whatever you want me too
I'm chilled right to the bone

Come with me the ghost did say
To a time you spent with family
When the season was much happier
Singing carols round the tree

A visit to the past all done
Ebenezer back in bed
When once again he heard a noise
He pulled the covers upon his head

Who is there? And what was that?
Ebenezer weakly cried
It's me the ghost of Christmas Now
There's no point in trying to hide

Leave me alone, I'm just an old man
You're scaring me half to death
The room was oh so cold and dark
Ebenezer could see his breath

Then with one small spark, a candle lit
The light chasing the darkness away
The ghost of Christmas Now stepped forth
We're gonna do things my way!

Come with me Ebenezer Scrooge
There are things that you must see
You need to learn that you must pay
Can't expect everything done for free!

A fair day's wage, for a fair day's work
Is one lesson you must learn
Or you'll one day stand at the gates of hell
And for eternity you'll burn

Once again Ebenezer cried
I'm listening and learning, oh please
As he held the robe of Christmas Now
And sobbing he sank to his knees

When Ebenezer opened his eyes again
He found himself back on his bed
With pictures of what he'd learnt so far
Tumbling around in his head

Then all at once from o'er the room
A sound Ebenezer heard
A shape it formed from shadows there
Looking very much like a bird

The shape it moved towards poor Scrooge
As out of the shadow it stepped
With a claw like hand it beckoned him
And near out his chest his heart leapt

Oh monstrous beast stay away from me
Scrooge begged as he fell on his knees
I'll change, I'll do whatever you want
Just don't hurt me, I'm begging you please

The bird-like Spectre bent down to Scrooge
As firmly he helped him to stand
He made to point the way to go
And lead him along by the hand

All at once Scrooge was to see
A grave all neglected and lonely
He knew before he saw the name
The grave would be his, and his only

Oh no cried Scrooge, please say it's not true
Then he noticed the date still to come
I promise I'll change my ways said he
Oh please Spectre, please take me home

Then with a whoosh he was in his bed
Back in his own bedroom
He swore that things were going to change
And made a plan there in the gloom

A Christmas morn dawned bright that day
Scrooge was filled with a new Christmas cheer
The folk who knew Ebenezer Scrooge
Could now live without any fear.........

Christmas

Bells on boughs and tinsel hung
Mince pies made and carols sung
Snow is falling thick and fast
Through the windows children gasp
Rosy cheeks and smiling faces
Stockings hung on fire places
Santa's coming, don't you worry
Off to bed the children scurry
Peace and quiet in the house
Nothing moving not a mouse

Then all at once a great big whoosh
'Whoa there boys just watch that bush!'
Reindeer settle on the ground
Father Christmas looks around
All is quiet in the street
'Let's get in and get some heat!'
By the tree the fire roars
Watch your step n don't bang doors!
Everyone is fast asleep
In each room he takes a peep
'Mince pie n milk, just what I need
A letter too, I'll have a read'

Dear Santa, I hope you've came,
For Christmas this year I'd like a game
I don't want a puzzle, or a bucking donkey
The dog eats the pieces, the donkey goes wonky!
The game that I'm after, as most of the nation
Is a well known game called frustration!
If you could do this I sure would be grateful
A biscuit's hidden, right under the table!
Enjoy your pie and warm your feet
I think the snow will be really deep!
Thank you so much for what you'll leave here
I hope you'll come back again next year!
With lots of hugs, hope it's not too chilly
Love and kisses, little Billy x

Santa smiles, a big friendly smile
It's letters like this make it worthwhile
Up from the chair, he moves to the tree
A present for mother and father he leaves
A doll and a pram for little Millie
Of course not forgetting a pressie for Billy!
Out through the door and into the night
Santa jumps on his sleigh and whispers goodnight!

A Happy New Year!

Another year, a fresh new start

I'll always love you, with all my heart

For family and friends, who have gone before

You're in my heart forever more

As the bells strike twelve, the clocks they chime

We'll raise a glass, for Auld Lang Syne

Family here, to those apart

Here's my wish, for the greatest start

A brand new year, to follow your dreams

Your hopes in life, what it means

New friends to meet, new family too

The New Year's here to welcome you!

So for those we've loved, for those we've lost

For those who can't be here

You're in my thoughts, as I raise a glass

And wish you all a HAPPY NEW YEAR!!!